Guilt Factors

Mind Games & Thought Nots!

ROBERT R. BLONDIN

Copyright © 2019 by Robert R. Blondin.

All rights reserved. No part of this publication may be reproduced, distributed, or transmitted in any form or by any means, including photocopying, recording, or other electronic or mechanical methods, without the prior written permission of the publisher, except in the case of brief quotations embodied in critical reviews and certain other noncommercial uses permitted by copyright law. For permission requests, write to the publisher, addressed "Attention: Permissions Coordinator," at the address below.

Narrative composition, poetry and artworks were created by the author and copyright laws hereby apply.

ARPress
45 Dan Road Suite 36
Canton MA 02021

Hotline: 1(800) 220-7660
Fax: 1(855) 752-6001

Ordering Information:
Quantity sales. Special discounts are available on quantity purchases by corporations, associations, and others. For details, contact the publisher at the address above.

Printed in the United States of America.

ISBN-13:   Hardback   979-8-89356-067-1

           eBook   979-8-89356-068-8

Library of Congress Control Number: 2024904001

CONTENTS

Preface v
Acknowledgment...vii
Dedication ix
Intro xi
Guilt Defined..xiii

Chapter 1. Guilt Factors..1
    Your mind, a wondrous & powerful thing! 2
    The brain, an immense intellectual power! 3
    Concealed memories! 4
    Mysteries of the mind! 5
    Guilt feelings - guilty complex!... 6
    Feelings, from guilt to déjà vu! 7
    Conscious awareness! 8
    Dreams - Nightmares! 9
    Conditioning the mind! 10
    Subconsciously speaking! 11
    Concentration to creativity! 12
    Delve into the talents within! 13
    The power within!..14
    Phenomenal things can happen! 15
    Perfect practice makes perfect! 16
    The mind, a powerful & complex machine, imagine! 17
    What part of the mind is really running the show! 18
    Subconscious Conclusion! 19

Chapter 2. Historical Quotes..21

Chapter 3. Poetry & Artworks..25
    The Pain 26
    Time, Only Time *(part one)* 28
    Time, Only Time *(part two)* 30
    Unseen Scars 32
    Home 34
    What My Eyes See 36
    If The Morning Doesn't Come...38

The Cottage 40
Shadow Of Darkness 42
Beyond The Unknown 44
Shadow Of Fear 46
Silent Waves 48
Love Can Hurt 50
The Visitors 52
Some Kind Of High 54
My Brother and I 56
The Reflection 58
A Ray Of Hope 60
The Depths Of Your Mind 62
Life Or Death? 64
From Beyond 66
Visions Drifting Through 68
Envision Me 70
Why? 72
Fortunate To Be One 74
Love's Pain 76
Fears Within *(part one)* 78
Fears Within *(part two)* 80
Wanting Her 82
Temper, Temper 84
Just A Face 86
Only You Can 88
Down and Out 90
Confusion! 92
For You I'll Wait 94
That Feeling 96
A Touch Of Golden *(An Ode To Mom & Dad)* 98
Return Journey 100

Chapter 4. Reader's Participation Page 101

Afterword 103

PREFACE

Permit yourself to wonder and to wander as we plunge into the known and the unknown through artwork and poetry.

*The forthcoming of morning is but the light of day,
the forthcoming of evening is but only the light taken away!*

Guilt Factors ~Mind Games & Thought Nots! starts with short motivational blurbs about guilt and the workings of the mind and is interlaced with poetry and artwork. It has a total of 4 chapters, including a poetic participation chapter, if one so chooses to analyze the poems.

- o *Guilt Factors*
- o *Historical Quotes*
- o *Poetry and Artworks*
- o *Participation Page*

ACKNOWLEDGMENT

These writings have been concocted, massaged and assembled over time, with the help, guidance and influence of so many people in my life, friends and family, and co-workers from the past.

It is with heartfelt thanks to all and hopefully you know who you all are, and, if not, at least I do.

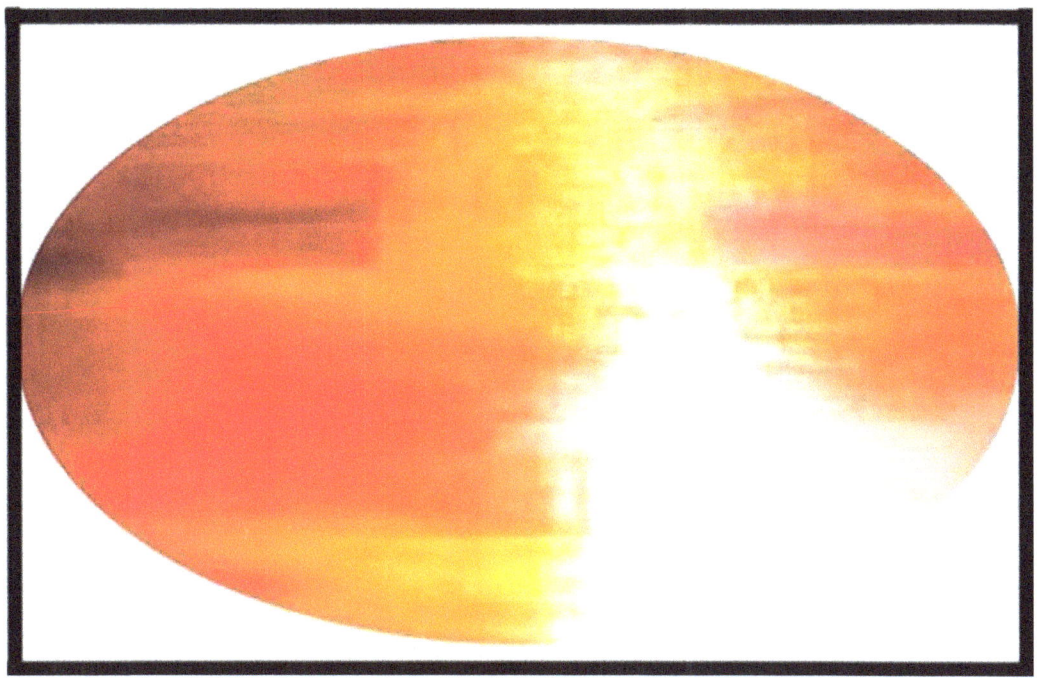

"I sometimes keep myself withdrawn from all and then I feel its presence known; it's very brief and brilliant ray, lets me know that my world is okay!"

DEDICATION

"Dedicated to dear family & friends"

A special shout out to my children, Kyle & Melinda and to my grandchildren, Austin, Nathaniel, Sydney Marie & Jake, and to those that may follow!

"Dream your dream, move some mountains,
believe in yourself,
be amazed at what you can accomplish,
what you can make others accomplish; age is irrelevant"

INTRO

Guilt Factors pertains to the intellect of one's being, the mind and the feelings spawned in varying situations of one's life, particularly guilt feelings and some factors involved, including positives and negatives; but mostly of an encouraging nature.

The content is by no means intended as a psychological validation or conclusions, only the writer's point of view, hence beware. And, it is by no means complete, only *short blurbs.*

The poetic ramblings contained herein are about life, its good days and bad days, with all its misunderstandings, mishaps and other unfortunate happenings, such as: personal loves, family loves, lost loves, drug abuse and misuse, pregnancies, abortions, attempt suicides, subsequent depressions, the unknown, futuristic beliefs, the darkness of death, and the ultimate, life after death.

Or – *it can be whatever you believe it to be!*

The substance of the poems is not necessarily the beliefs or the feelings of the author and are only poetic summaries of what my mind has imagined, what my eyes have seen, what my ears have heard and, yes, what my heart has felt. *And of course, what I've just conjured up!*

They say the brain can play 'mind games' on you, with good thoughts, evil thoughts, and the dreaded thought nots, thus the sub-title *"Mind Games & 'ought Nots!" Always believe in yourself, you can do it.*

Artwork by this author has been added to offset any feelings of guilt, shame or shivering flashbacks to your past, but then again who knows.

GUILT DEFINED

Guilt is something everyone has; those amazing inner feelings experienced within one's lifetime; something each and every one of us will become aware of at some point in life, whether we like it or not!

These ramblings contain passages describing elements of guilt and other related subjects dealing with the mind, all from the author's perspective, a layman at best, therefore I find it important to purposely give a short definition of 'guilt' here, as it is officially documented in some realms.

Here are 3 types of guilt:

- *Healthy* or real guilt is when you know you've done something wrong. It's our conscience telling us that we have done something against our morals and beliefs. It's a natural process of evaluating one's self in the light of honesty.

- *Unhealthy* guilt occurs when you feel everything is your fault – even things totally beyond your control.

- *False* guilt applies to those who have been victims of abuse or violent crimes, yet they feel it was their fault to some degree.

Some, all or none may apply to these writings, you be the judge.

I'm sure there are other types of guilt too – they just keep giving things bigger names, like essential guilt, deserved guilt, self-generated guilt, borrowed guilt, hindsight guilt, and so on.

CHAPTER 1

GUILT FACTORS

Mind Games & Thought Nots!

YOUR MIND, A WONDROUS & POWERFUL THING!

Your mind is a wondrous and powerful thing, controlling your destiny, from day one onward through a life cycle of self-being, then returning to where it all began.

During the journey, you'll experience many feelings, some great and some not so great; hence the old adage, "that's life".

Your own mind is a complex and powerful machine. It is capable of making you do anything you deem to be possible.

More importantly, you are able to make it do almost anything.

Yes, anything?

The mind controls your thoughts, your emotions, and subsequently your impending destiny.

THE BRAIN, AN IMMENSE INTELLECTUAL POWER!

The brain itself is a highly intricate organ and an immense intellectual power.

The mind contains a conscious component, with your mental faculties being awake and a subconscious component, not fully cognizant or awake, but still functions taking in everything you see, feel and hear, even without you actually knowing it.

Most people simply believe they are not capable of attaining certain heights of success, no matter what it might be. is is mainly because they do not allow their mind to resolve their problems or use it to its full potential to attain their goal.

Knowledge takes time to age, just as you do.

Even if you are quite young, you are able to do things not thought of at such a tender age. is is usually unknown to them though, since this knowledge is stored strictly in the mind, where it sits dormant awaiting some kind of prompt, from the conscious side of the mind or influenced by others.

CONCEALED MEMORIES!

Everything you forget is not really forgotten; it is only concealed in your subconscious. It eventually will come to the surface and, thus, you remember what you had supposedly forgotten.

This is very similar to what can be construed as memory retention; this, more so, is the lack of memory skills wherein the mind just blocks it out, like a brain cramp.

Eventually, if you keep trying to remember, it will come back to you.

Your mind grows with knowledge as you grow. Everyone is inflicted with it and most do not even know they have it.

Such vast information lies beyond your normal awareness level, waiting to be conjured to the surface. It just waits dormant and can, unfortunately, remain as such throughout your whole life.

MYSTERIES OF THE MIND!

Thoughts from your subconscious tend to surface every few minutes and usually without warning.

They can be good thoughts, bad thoughts or a mixture.

This usually occurs when you allow your mind to wander, similar to daydreaming.

The mind contains many mysteries.

Sometimes your thoughts can be about things, places or people you haven't seen or heard of in years, and some you don't even remember ever seeing or hearing of before.

Everyone is controlled by his or her own mind.

Feelings and emotions can develop into what is known as guilt and/or depression, but you and your mind also control the severity of it.

It can create varied attitudes and personalities amongst people and sometimes remains festered within one's self, transparent to them, but not to others.

GUILT FEELINGS - GUILTY COMPLEX!

Guilt is defined mostly as having committed an implied offence, a feeling of culpability or a mental obsession with the idea of having done a wrong.

The definition of guilt is not necessarily a truth.

You may only think you have done a wrong, hence the creation of a guilt complex.

Guilt feelings can be caused by something deep within your subconscious and can be contained as such even when you haven't done anything wrong at all.

Your guilt feelings may in fact be just something you have imagined at one point in time.

You therefore could be subjecting yourself to what you believe is guilt, but may only be a form of insecurity or second guessing on your part and not guilt at all.

This is being inflicted upon you by the powers of your mind.

FEELINGS, FROM GUILT TO DÉJÀ VU!

Depression is mostly defined as a state of morbidly excessive melancholy, a mood of hopelessness and feelings of inadequacy, often with physical symptoms.

This also is not necessarily a truth.

As with guilt, you again may only be subjecting yourself to these feelings, thus being under the unwanted controls of your subconscious mind.

You can learn to control your own mind and its many wonders and secrets.

Most people don't believe this to be true or even possible, but yes you can invoke some form of control.

It's all up to the individual; this means you.

Have you ever seen or heard something and have sworn you have seen it or heard it somewhere before?

It's uncanny how the mind works; is the thought process just distorting your senses?

Is it déjà vu or something from the realm of the unknown?

CONSCIOUS AWARENESS!

Yes, déjà vu maybe, but, not really, then again who is to say.

What was that strange feeling of knowing that place, being there before?

Déjà vu anyone? Not really, but then again who is to say.

Most likely it's because of something that has been stored in your subconscious mind without you even realizing it.

It was more than likely outside your conscious awareness the first time.

Of course, there could be other unexplainable reasons; well, couldn't there be?

Maybe what you've seen, heard or felt, was within the supernatural realm, perhaps magic, perhaps clairvoyance, perhaps the twilight zone or maybe, just maybe, the powers above.

Well, perhaps!!?

These, however, are things most people do not believe in or simply are afraid to believe in.

Therefore, let's simply blame it on our subconscious mind for these happenings, be they strange, wacky or wonderful.

DREAMS - NIGHTMARES!

Dreams and even nightmares are a creation of the mind.

Have you ever dreamt of something realizing that never in a thousand years could you have imagined such a thing.

Just maybe your subconscious mind has seen it somewhere before.

Have you ever had repetitive dreams, night after night?

You obviously have wondered why and sought out a reasonable explanation for them. Did you arrive at a logical conclusion?

Some people do manage to find the answer realizing that at one time earlier in their lives they had experienced a similar occurrence or had listened to some other persons happening and have subsequently dreamt of it as if it was actually themselves involved.

Some people however cannot find the answers.

These people either continue to dream the dream or the dream has subsided on its own.

Hopefully it was the latter.

CONDITIONING THE MIND!

The subconscious mind can play many tricks on you, so it's up to you and only you, to condition it accordingly, day in and day out.

Ever hear of suggestive thinking?

This is a form of control, which you can eventually condition your mind to do and it is solely controlled by your thoughts.

An example would be sleeping problems, which a vast number of people tend to have for whatever reasons.

You can condition yourself to sleep at whatever time and to awake at whatever time, by repeating the commands to your brain.

Unbeknownst to you, these commands are stored in your subconscious and, believe it or not, will work just like an alarm clock.

But, like I said, you must continue the conditioning until it takes effect and works for you.

Some people are unsuccessful in their attempts; however it might only be a direct lack of trying or believing on their part.

Like anything else, what works for others doesn't necessarily mean it will work for you.

SUBCONSCIOUSLY SPEAKING!

They say, 'once a skeptic, always a skeptic'.

It's up to you; when it comes to the mind, believe what you will.

Remember, it's not always what you know, it's how you use what you know and in turn, use what your mind knows within the subconscious.

You must develop or condition it to react to your thinking.

You shouldn't simply react to your thoughts.

You must try for control, and keep in mind (forgive the pun), your mind is two parts working together, although one is supposedly dormant, this being your subconscious, which can come to the surface (the conscious part) very quickly and also disappear just as quickly.

It will even occasionally surface to interfere with your present thoughts and that is why it is very important to develop your mind to do what you want it to do or think.

Come on now, let's try to concentrate!

CONCENTRATION TO CREATIVITY!

Concentration can be key.

This is why people tend to keep a pen or pencil handy for writing their thoughts down during a conversation with others or during times when others are talking, be it in person, the television noise, radio noise or whatever.

The subconscious can store an enormous amount of information unbeknownst to you and therefore can sometimes hold you in captivity because you may never ever come to realize that vast reserve of knowledge.

And, such a pity!

While you are awake or conscious, you are not supposed to dream, however we have all heard of daydreamers, haven't we, maybe even been one.

Believe it or not, some of the most creative people are those who tend to be either daydreamers or actual people who become creative through their dreams during sleep.

DELVE INTO THE TALENTS WITHIN!

People seem to say that those of us, who are inventors, playwrights, and the like, are talented and gifted.

Maybe they actually are, but it's not always because they are naturally gifted or brilliant.

It could be because they've somehow learned to use their minds effectively and to the fullest extent, and believed in themselves.

Isn't it obvious that some don't?

Even when you sleep, the mind still works and creates ideas and images or dreams, and, yes, sometimes nightmares!

People from all walks of life have all envisioned their accomplishments or greatness during sleep and have awakened to fulfill their dreams; well, okay, some have, some haven't.

Perhaps even you can do it, no matter how small or how big the undertaking might be.

THE POWER WITHIN!

Maybe you have already been the fortunate one to have reached your goal, once maybe, however not continuously.

This is what you must attain on a regular basis, but most cannot or simply won't.

That might be the reason for so many frustrated people out there; those who think they don't have talent period or those that show talent but just don't succeed in their endeavors.

I am sure there are a lot of underlying reasons for someone's lack of success; however it might help if they learn to use the complete knowledge that is stored in their subconscious, to eventually overcome any or most obstacles in their path.

The mind can create mysteries and stumbling blocks but it can solve them too, if you just think hard enough!

Try, try, and keep on trying in order to succeed.

Oh, the power we have within!

PHENOMENAL THINGS CAN HAPPEN!

Conditioning the mind and self-programming are very similar in that both deal with the mind in some way.

Conditioning the mind is what I've spoken of and self-programming is much the same but it is also relative to the use of the body itself.

You can make the body do amazing things too but again it is the mind that controls the actions.

Have you ever heard of people who have lifted things of immense weight in an attempt to get the heavy object off a loved one, such as a jacked up car that falls on someone?

You know basically that it is impossible for you to do this but during the anxiety or stress of the situation, you do it anyways and suddenly the car rises.

How did you do it? How could you do it?

Who really knows the answers to that but perhaps the mind and body worked together to create this amazing phenomenon, the mind giving the body muscle power beyond belief.

PERFECT PRACTICE MAKES PERFECT!

Ever heard of the term visualization?

Again, it is very similar to conditioning and self-programming as mentioned earlier.

You have heard of how people will try to psyche themselves up before an event takes place, haven't you? Visualization is a big part of it; however, it must be used properly to take its fullest effect and reap success.

All you do, or should do, is visualize your accomplishments ahead of time, in some mental shape or form, and on an ongoing basis until your mind has been conditioned to control your bodily functions to the letter of success.

This may take time but it will work for anything at all you wish to undertake, whether it be sports or otherwise.

This method is known to succeed for even those of a young age, with assistance from a mentor.

Simply visualize what you have to do, repetitively, and eventually you will be able to do so, at least to some degree.

Remember an old adage, 'practice makes perfect' or perhaps even better, 'perfect practice makes perfect'!!

THE MIND, A POWERFUL & COMPLEX MACHINE, IMAGINE!

As said before, the mind is a wondrous and powerful thing.

It can think, dream, create and imagine things, true, false or otherwise.

It makes you what you are, what you'll eventually be. Yes, you can develop it to make you more than what you are, more than you ever dreamed possible.

Have you ever heard of people who live in the past and those that simply live day to day; perhaps even those who live in the future.

Flashbacks to the past and thinking of the future are important factors in the growth of the mind, whether it is contained in the conscious part of your brain or the subconscious part.

The mind – such a complex and powerful machine.

Just think about it!!

WHAT PART OF THE MIND IS REALLY RUNNING THE SHOW!

Most people believe that consciousness in itself is the one part of the mind we actually think with. Yet, it comprises only a small part of the mind, and believe it or not, it more than likely is the least important part.

The subconscious mind on the other hand is really running the show for the most part and is evident in almost everything we tend to do.

Even though the subconscious is amazingly powerful, it is not almighty.

It is changeable to some degree and you and only you, control its great power.

You can, oh yes you can!

SUBCONSCIOUS CONCLUSION!

"Your mind controls your thoughts, your emotions, and your impending destiny".

All I ask is that you take the time to consider all the aforementioned factors and seriously think about it.

Believe in yourself!

Who knows, you might just be able to move mountains with your dreams and I wouldn't really mind!

The ensuing poems may well cover some of the subjects outlined in the foregoing – or not!

"Dream your dream,
move those mountains,
believe in yourself,
be amazed at what you can accomplish,
what you can make others accomplish;
and remember, age is irrelevant".

CHAPTER 2

HISTORICAL QUOTES

Before you get to the poetic and artworks section of Guilt Factors, here are a few historical quotes to ponder when it comes to guilt and the workings of the mind.

We are shaped by our thoughts; we become what we think. When the mind is pure, joy follows like a shadow that never leaves.
Buddha
(Sage - ?400 BCE?)

When the mind is thinking, it is talking to itself.
Plato
(Philosopher - ?430 BCE?)

Whatever the mind of man can conceive and believe, it can achieve.
W. Clement Stone
(American Self Help Author – Born: May 4, 1902 Died: September 3, 2002)

To accomplish great things, we must not only act, but also dream; not only plan, but also believe.
Anatole France
(French Poet and Novelist – Born: April 16, 1844 Died: October 12, 1924)

It's strange indeed how memories can lie dormant in a man's mind for so many years. Yet those memories can be awakened and brought forth fresh and new, just by something you've seen, or something you've heard, or the sight of an old familiar face.
Wilson Rawls
(American Novelist – Born: September 24, 1913 Died: December 16, 1984)

All our dreams can come true, if we have the courage to pursue them.
Walt Disney
(American animator, cartoonist, producer, director, screenwriter and voice actor, born: December 5, 1901 Died: December 15, 1966)

The worst guilt is to accept an unearned guilt.
Ayn Rand
(American Novelist – Born: February 2, 1905 Died: March 6, 1982)

Hard though it may be to accept, remember that guilt is sometimes a friendly internal voice reminding you that you're messing up.
Marge Kennedy
(American Author)

I have never smuggled anything in my life. Why, then, do I feel an uneasy sense of guilt on approaching a customs barrier?
John Steinbeck
(Author – Born: February 27, 1902 Died: December 20, 1968)

There's no regret. You can't regret. I mean, I've felt regret but I've also refused to allow regret to sow a seed and live in me because I don't believe it. You feel it, it's like guilt, it's like jealousy, it's like all those horrible things. You've just got to snip them and get them out, because they're no good.
Jude Law
(British Actor)

We all feel the urge to condemn ourselves out of guilt, to blame others for our misfortunes and to fantasize about total disaster.
Deepak Chopra
(American Philosopher)

Guilt is anger directed at ourselves – at what we did or did not do. Resentment is anger directed at others – at what they did or did not do.
Peter McWilliams
(American Self-Help Author – Born: August 5, 1949 Died: June 14, 2000)

My guiding principle is this: Guilt is never to be doubted.
Franz Kafka
(Novelist – Born: July 3, 1883 Died: June 3, 1924)

Life is one big road with lots of signs. So when you are riding through the ruts, don't complicate your mind. Flee from hate, mischief and jealousy. Don't bury your thoughts, put your vision to reality. Wake Up and Live!
Bob Marley
(Musician – Born: February 6, 1945 Died: May 11, 1981)

As to the pure mind all things are pure, so to the poetic mind all things are poetical.
Henry Wadsworth Longfellow
(Poet – February 27, 1807 – March 24, 1882)

Peace is but the subsiding of pain, hurt is but the creation of guilt, guilt is but only a feeling, deep within the subconscious being.
Robert R. Blondin

CHAPTER 3

POETRY & ARTWORKS

~ artwork has no bearing on poems or vice versa ~

THE PAIN

"Peace is but the subsiding of pain,
Hurt is but the creation of guilt,
Guilt is but only a feeling,
Deep within the subconscious being"

Marie – RIP

TIME, ONLY TIME
(part one)

Nothing but time,
a circular motion in life,
changing and rearranging,
here awaiting destiny.

Caressing each breath I have,
still hoping for more,
nothing but time,
just awaiting the end.

Cylinders of darkness,
tunnels of light,
peaking to the inevitable,
the circular motion of life,
nothing but time,
only time.

Seconds pass,
then the sound of broken glass,
the shattering of time,
inflicting a sharp jagged pain,
leaving an aching in my heart,
that just won't seem to pass.

Sails In Thee Golden Red Sky

TIME, ONLY TIME
(part two)

Falling into slow motion,
with a sudden thud,
caught in the hands of time,
unable to converse,
now charred with fear; then,
the sounds of footsteps near.

Cylinders of darkness, tunnels of light, spiraling shadows,
in and out of sight.

Now, I'm surrounded by an aura,
a mysterious aura, with a smell,
the scent of fresh cut flowers, yet,
encircling the presence of fear.

And so, I remain here, bound by time, nothing but time.

Only time.

Bluestream

UNSEEN SCARS

Childish schemes, scattered dreams,
Everlasting feelings, unseen scars,
Still dormant in the dark canyons of my mind,
slowly garnered, through the ages of time.

A stretching imagination,
infectious in itself,
Now scattered and running amok,
My spirit slightly numbed.

Deep feelings emerging,
surfacing, dangling and dancing,
as if jumping from an old dusty book.

Childish schemes, scattered dreams,
Everlasting feelings, unseen scars.

Devilish

HOME

It sure wasn't much,
But we called it home,
Mom and Dad had twelve kids,
So no one was ever alone.

We all got by with what we had,
Times were hard but also quite glad,
We all shared what there was,
Hand-me-downs, on top of all the love.

Yes, so poor we were but love was always there,
Respect and admiration everywhere.
It sure wasn't much,
no prosperity as such,
but we called it home.

Mom and Dad had twelve kids,
So no one was ever alone.

Golden Blue Grass

WHAT MY EYES SEE

I shall always cry,
because my eyes see life as a lie.

Each sorrow or great happiness,
Is only what we scrounge,
beg or borrow.

To live a life is not to rest,
beyond is what we shall truly live.

A wondrous, glorious sight,
pure, crystal and natural as light.

Heather & Randy, caricature

IF THE MORNING DOESN'T COME

If the morning doesn't come,
and your day turns to night,
I'll be there to make it alright.

When you are down and lonely,
and the feeling of life has gone,
I'll be over to sing a sweet song.

If your heart becomes broken,
and need soft words spoken,
I'll be there, 'cause I care.

If your morning doesn't come,
and your day turns to night,
I'll be there to hold you real tight.

If you see your path getting weary,
don't quite know what you'll find,
I'll show you the way,
For I am yours and you are mine.

If you need love and affection,
I'll put you in the right direction;
If you can't find what you seek,
and darkness fills the air,
stay with me, I'll help you search,
you know how much I care.

If the morning doesn't come,
and your day turns to night,
I'll always be there,
making it alright.

Midnight Sail

THE COTTAGE

Trees swaying in the cool breeze,
Branches staying in tune with the leaves;
Nearby, a little brook calmly flowing,
Along the side, wild flowers growing,
The surroundings enhanced with love,
Expectations far and above,
Time for seclusion without confusion,
The cottage, a nice location,
With no provocation.

Sometimes life throws you a curve, sometimes just too much to bear, so sometimes you just have to get away.

Old Sideroad North

SHADOW OF DARKNESS

The forthcoming of darkness,
the coming of death,
gliding slowly down the trail,
searching for my place of rest.

Floating through the lonely,
dark secluded passages,
as the stillness closes in,
the memories slowly emerge,
what I've done, where I've been;
then the shadow of darkness,
... of death!

Regatta's Blur

BEYOND THE UNKNOWN

Reasoning beyond doubt,
Outer limits unseen,
Inner planetary objects,
swirling and jutting out.
The dark horizons yet unearthed,
Ghastly experiments being secretly researched,
wondering who will be first.
The forthcoming of light,
the utter darkness of the night,
with creations beyond thought,
the world as it is and is not.
Amazed and bewildered
at how it all began,
the evolution of man,
does anyone really know,
can anyone begin to understand.
Although the great book has been written,
the real truth, the only truth,
is not known, or has it been overblown.
is world just keeps growing,
populations exploding,
rivers and oceans overflowing,
and nobody really knowing.

Blue Brush Cave

SHADOW OF FEAR

Her eyes were a glittering green,
with a bewildering gleam,
her hair was a golden hue,
damp with a light touch of morning dew.

She stood in a shadow of her own making,
as if there for the taking,
the air had a scent of the wild,
but yet, with a temperament, quite mild.

She raised her hand, motioning me forward,
I made a step, but froze, like a coward,
I could sense an evil near, but my eyes could not see,
and I could not hear.

I felt the excitement she created,
the thrill she instilled in me,
she was a silhouette outline, in the narrow path ahead,
her piercing eyes paralyzing me;
all my senses now dead.

Unconsciously I approached, with a cautious step,
I knew I could not turn back, not now,
not ever, not yet.

Her arms stretched out, embracing my soul,
my excitement grew, and then withdrew, and
then, everything went cold, she had hold.

The Sunset

SILENT WAVES

Silent waves, the solemn soft wind blowing,
clear blue water flowing,
seeing a vision of her on the sandy shore,
but now disappearing, to be seen no more.

Suddenly a nasty cool wind appears,
creating a fortress in the sand;
and from the formed gritty mound,
comes the formation of a hand,
stretching, reaching out, grasping
for fulfillment.

Fear instills my already trembling body,
as the hand surges upward and forward,
slowly approaching my soul,
coming closer, closer, and closer,
grasping for a piece of me,
a small piece of reality.

An inner sense suddenly emerges
and destroys my thinking,
both reality and non-reality now linking,
as I open my eyes to the silent waves, and
the solemn soft wind blowing.

Beach Side Bush

LOVE CAN HURT

Never would I ever,
fall in love again,
never would I ever,
glance at your picture again,
its hidden in a drawer,
to be seen no more.

I loved you so much,
to caress, hold and touch,
your loving smile,
your kiss, so luscious,
but yet amiss, and all the while,
you left leaving me in vain,
driving me slowly insane.

Never would I ever,
fall in love again,
Never would I ever,
glance at your picture again;
no valid reasons given,
you just up and went,
so what's the purpose of living,
my times all used, all spent;
never would I ever,
fall in love again.

Falling out of love can be agonizing, filled with doubt, guilt and anxiety.
It can even be more emotional than falling in love.

Fireburst

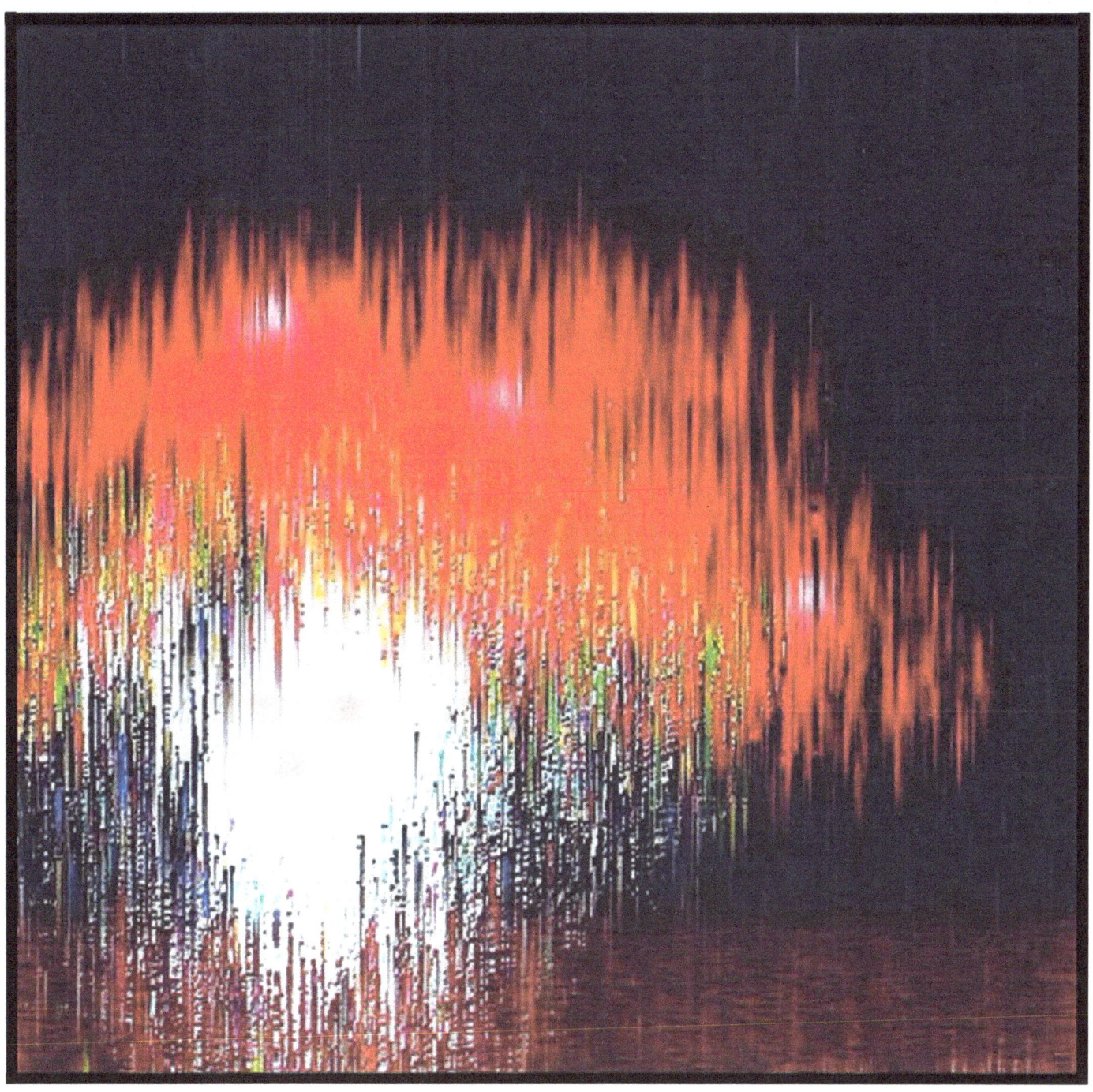

THE VISITORS

We come to you in thoughts,
sometimes quickly, sometimes not.

We stay as long as we want,
or, as long as you want;

We sometimes even haunt,
maybe just taunt.

We survive in memories, good or bad,
you control the emotion,
whatever the notion,
it's not a magic potion.

We sometimes appear as magical orbs,
Sometimes shadows, white or black,
just to give you a shivering flashback.

We come to you in thoughts,
sometimes quickly, sometimes not.

Firestorm Reflected

SOME KIND OF HIGH

Perspective dreams,
with cowardly schemes.

Sudden characteristics changing,
lives shuffed and rearranging.

Pictorial patterns, filled with golden Saturns,
and pixilated people vividly feeble.

Just fabrications of mine,
concepts and visual memories,
caught up in a quandary of time,
and so drastically benign.

Oh, it was some kind of high!

I swear I never ever ever inhaled …

The Simpsons

Mario's Snooze

MY BROTHER AND I

My brother and I ...
Only heaven keeps us parted;
But somehow I feel restrained,
And still I remain,
here where I started.

Being one with one
is not to run;
Look into my eyes for
I'm no spy;
And, if you should cry,
you'll realize why, Be
calm my brother, to me
we'll live forever.

Greeting is our eternal gift,
Goodbye is nothing to our mind's eye,
Love is what holds us together;
We'll meet again, only to begin,
Yes, my brother, to begin.

Snow Mountain

THE REFLECTION

Into a mirror I gaze,
the lone figure drifting into haze,
a reflection of life;
the dark image comes into view,
that image of death itself.

The innerness of my being,
touching, clutching my very soul;
the reflection surges forward,
standing out like it was
borrowed; visualizing into life,
into utter realization.

With one last hope of courage,
I reach to destroy it,
that dark reflective image,
but as my flesh touches the cold aura, a
flashing bright haloed light shines and
emerges, emitting the final calling.

Extreme Sunset Reflected

A RAY OF HOPE

In the mysterious depths of my mind,
its wondrous spirits fly.

My consciousness reaps and sows,
my mind absorbs the tolls,
my soul hides deep, does not sleep.

I stay withdrawn, something is gnawing,
yet I feel it's presence known,
something is glowing.

It's very brief and brilliant ray,
tells me that my world is surely okay!

*No matter how bad it may get for you, no matter how dreary,
no matter how dark, never give up on hope, never say never.*

Stormy Sunset

THE DEPTHS OF YOUR MIND

Drifting fever of love,
Everlasting feelings,
Through the ages of time,
Holding onto only a fraction that is mine.

Awaiting the deafening sound,
Yet to hear and find,
Knowing the thunderous shaking,
The pounding in your mind.

Widening landscapes of the universe,
Unkind and treacherous people,
All just making it worse.

Your stretching imagination running away,
Deep within the non-reality of thought,
Seeing the world as it is and is not,
Happiness, wishfulness,
And then, the unsaid death, silence.

To be at peace within the saneness of life,
The reality of being, the true reality of life;
Sometimes the answer is just too hard,
Too hard to find knowing the guilt,
The guilt within the depths of your mind!

Some people carry grudges, bathe themselves in hatred or linger in guilt, for years on end, never ever coming to rest with their inner feelings. Oh so sad! Let your positive thoughts outshine the negatives and you can accomplish whatever you so desire; it may take a lot of effort, constant effort, but you'll dream your dream one day!

Night Owl

LIFE OR DEATH?

The cutting off of Life.
The dullness of a shrieking cold knife.
The hurt, the everlasting scar.
Outdoing the pain of life by far.

Abortion, you think?

Lonesome Pines

FROM BEYOND

Beckoning calls from beyond,
The deafening shrieking noise,
engulfing my soul, my mind,
My golden silence now gone.

The shrieking noise thrusts forward,
reaching out, clutching, wrestling,
slicing through the thin air;
the ensuing gust turns me about;
leaving me in hopeless despair.

Within the whispers of the cool breeze,
I can hear the sounds imposing,
the beckoning sounds enclosing,
those shuttering calls from beyond,
such an eerie feeling, an eerie tone,
my senses all gone, now all alone.

Cocco – Glamarosso

VISIONS DRIFTING THROUGH

Your face, your smile,
visions drifting through,
I forgot not to remember you.
A whispering breeze mentions your name,
slowly, agonizingly, driving me insane.
The beauty of your smile,
your long flowing hair,
visions drifting through,
I forgot not to remember you.
You're with me, inside me,
As I walk, you walk,
as I talk, you talk,
visions drifting through,
I forgot not to remember you.
Your loveliness caresses my soul, as the mystics unfold,
your spiritual presence,
apparent and reaching out,
now touching, feeling, existing,
you're with me, inside me,
And all because I forgot,
I forgot not to remember you.

I See You

ENVISION ME

Envision me,
Visualize my being,
Suspended in time,
Caress the aura,
The sensation benign,
Envision me,
Touch my soul,
Envision me,
Here I am, floating in time.

Sails In The Golden Sky

WHY?

Inner feelings creeping,
loving tears seeping,
glaring, glimmering eyes upon you,
holding back the tears,
for a man does not cry,
don't ask the reasons why,
it's something grown in a man,
since way back when;
a man's feelings should never be expressed,
never second-guessed;
a leader and protector he must be,
the tears we should not see,
for if he does weep and cry,
he must give excuses, reasons why.
Inner feelings creeping,
loving eyes seeping,
glaring eyes upon you ... why?

In some cultures, if not most, old fashioned concepts never die, do they?
It is quite normal for a man to cry when he loses a loved one, a loved pet, when he gets married, when he becomes a father or when he totals his very first car, or as far as I'm concerned, whenever he wants to!

Lexi – RIP

FORTUNATE TO BE ONE

Times are hard and times are tough,
Be happy, you've got more than some,
Yet, wishing and hoping for more,
But no one ever has enough.
Be fortunate to be one,
To be one with one is not to run,
You are damn fortunate to be one.
is ever changing world we live in,
Your life rearranging, melodies playing,
Reaching for the utmost,
Remember, don't boast, just coast,
People make their own lives,
With Fathers, Mothers, Sons and Daughters,
Husbands and Wives;
To be one with one is not to run,
You're fortunate to be one.
Your life is your life,
But don't forget, others have a share,
So, don't take it away,
Others care, they really do care,
To be one with one is not to run,
Yes, you're damn fortunate to be one!

Some days, just staying alive is the most important thing on your mind, except when dark thoughts approach and take over your mind and soul, and so, you lose all control. Remember one thing though; you are damn fortunate to be who you are, fortunate to be one

Whiskers – RIP

LOVE'S PAIN

Creation is but the pain of ecstasy,
The suffering you must bear;
You can surely see, by eying your past,
The shame doesn't have to last and last,
Be at peace with thy soul;
Accept, care and share,
Don't carry life and offer revenge,
The birth of life is what we yearn,
And to err is but to learn.
Nothing is quite the same as 'love's pain',
The great feeling of new life,
One within one.
So, don't carry life and offer revenge,
Your actions were but hardcore dramatics,
An immature reason for getting your kicks.
Reach out for a warm hand,
An understanding heart,
a kind and gentle soul.
Don't carry life and yet offer revenge.
And who am I? I'm but a friend!

Crystal Pines

FEARS WITHIN
(part one)

The danger erupts,
the unknown thrusts forward;
the invisible twine, entangling,
tightening, choking, strangling,
Gasping for air, all in utter despair.

Fears within;
the unknown remains unknown!

Wanting the simple truth,
craving the inevitable,
Seeking the realism of life,
the awakening of life,
Searching for a true tomorrow,
the future of mankind.

Fears within;
the unknown remains unknown!

Does it?

Whoami?

FEARS WITHIN
(part two)

Reaching into the emptiness,
the openness of outer space,
editing tomorrow's headlines,
knowing the unsaid predictions,
seeing errors not yet made.

Fears within;
the unknown remains unknown!

Watching life's tragic trail,
a heart stopping fail,
hearing earthquakes not yet erupting,
Speaking words not yet known,
or never ever spoken
Feeling the pain still to be felt.

Fears within;
the unknown remains unknown!

Does it?

Sunburst

WANTING HER

Where did I go wrong,
Am I not where I belong,
What has happened to my mind.

I seem to be wandering,
dreaming in a past time;
maybe I'm just wishing,
hoping I was back there,
in a time, so young, so in love,
with the one
I cherished, far and above.

Or, am I slowly losing my mind,
sweet memories of the girl,
the love once mine.

It use to be so clear,
so vivid in my mind,
wanting her, needing her,
yet knowing I'll never have her.

Wanting her but not getting,
so long ago, all in a past time,
but all within my mind.

The Night's Purple Haze

TEMPER, TEMPER

So calm and sentimental I tried to be,
but it surged forward, started strangling me.

The guilt I had inside, too hard to conceal;
emotional outbursts, loss of control,
no longer did I have a sense of real.

What is this, what do I feel?

It gushed outwardly, flowing quite free,
nothing can stop the onslaught;
maybe only me.

It heaped to the top, hot, hot, hot,
it would not be suppressed,
it could not be stopped.

Temper, temper.

Losing one's temper…

I think they now call it 'Intermittent Explosive Disorder' (or 'IED').

Umm…

Lonesome Wolf

JUST A FACE

Within a mirror you see but a face,
Within your mind not a trace,
The reverse reflection does not reveal,
A blank picture of how you really feel.

Seeing a vision of nothing living,
No sense of what the image is giving,
It's just a face, without a trace,
Amid a glancing look into space.

Into the mirror you visualize,
Take a closer look, maybe you'll realize,
Seeing a vision of nothing living,
Just a face, just a face,
An utter waste.

Baretrees

ONLY YOU CAN

I have seen the sign,
seen your kind,
nothing will stop me now.

I have felt the hurt,
felt my face ground into dirt,
nothing will stop me now.

I have known your likes
and your dislikes, known
how high you set your sights,
nothing will stop me now.

I have been there before,
been able to face the chore,
nothing will stop me now.

I have known the sensations,
known the provocations,
nothing will stop me now.

I have known love,
known how it is to be well above,
nothing will stop me now.

No, nothing will stop me now,
Only you can.

Jess

DOWN AND OUT

Another day of utter loneliness,
nothing ever going right;
it can all be said by the stillness,
the silence of the night.

Here I am, down and out,
and there is absolutely no doubt,
I don't know what it's all about.

Seeing visions of nothing, hearing
whispered words spoken, feeling
down and quite heartbroken.

The subdued aura, the quietness,
the silence inflicting my mind,
I'm pondering over what's to be,
What's left behind.

Here I am, down and out,
absolutely no doubt,
I don't know what it's all about.

Stay Positive, never ever give up!

Redmoon

CONFUSION!

From a painter's point of view,
the picture on the wall said it all.

The curves and strokes of the brush,
vibrating a titillating rush.

The vibrant color fast designs,
with protuberant lines and shades of hue,
creating a perspective quite anew.

But only a case of fiction, not fact.

And, if thou art confused,
It must be abstract!!

Austin?

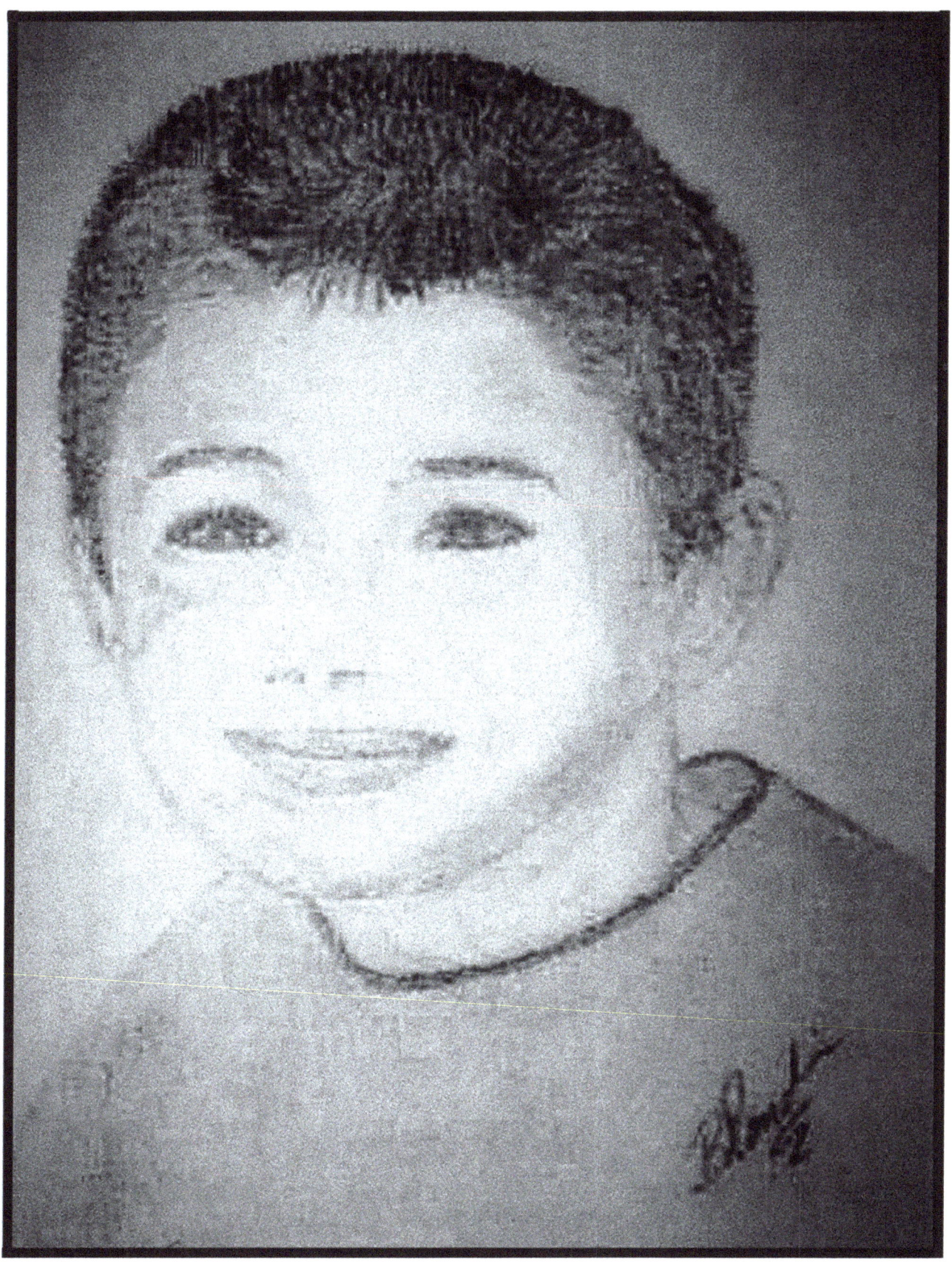

FOR YOU I'LL WAIT

A song in my heart
and no one to listen.

Longing, waiting and hoping,
for what?

I'm empty, I'm stiff;
my heart keeps pounding,
feelings running adrift.

Visions sad and visions glad;
not sure what I have,
what I might have had.

Where am I? What am I?

Here alone, not quite content,
hollow, incomplete and spent;
bring to me the one I love,
we'll sing our love song,
until the day we're gone.

Hold me, touch me,
breathe for me, with me,
caress my soul, be with me.

For you I'll wait,
my strength is great.

Deep Cold Contemplation

THAT FEELING

To see the hurt approaching,
  knowing what to expect.

To wander through the darkness,
  to feel the never-ending pain.

To want what can never be yours,
  To feel the sorrow once again.

Pain ... a feeling that slowly ceases!

Mom GrammaB 2007

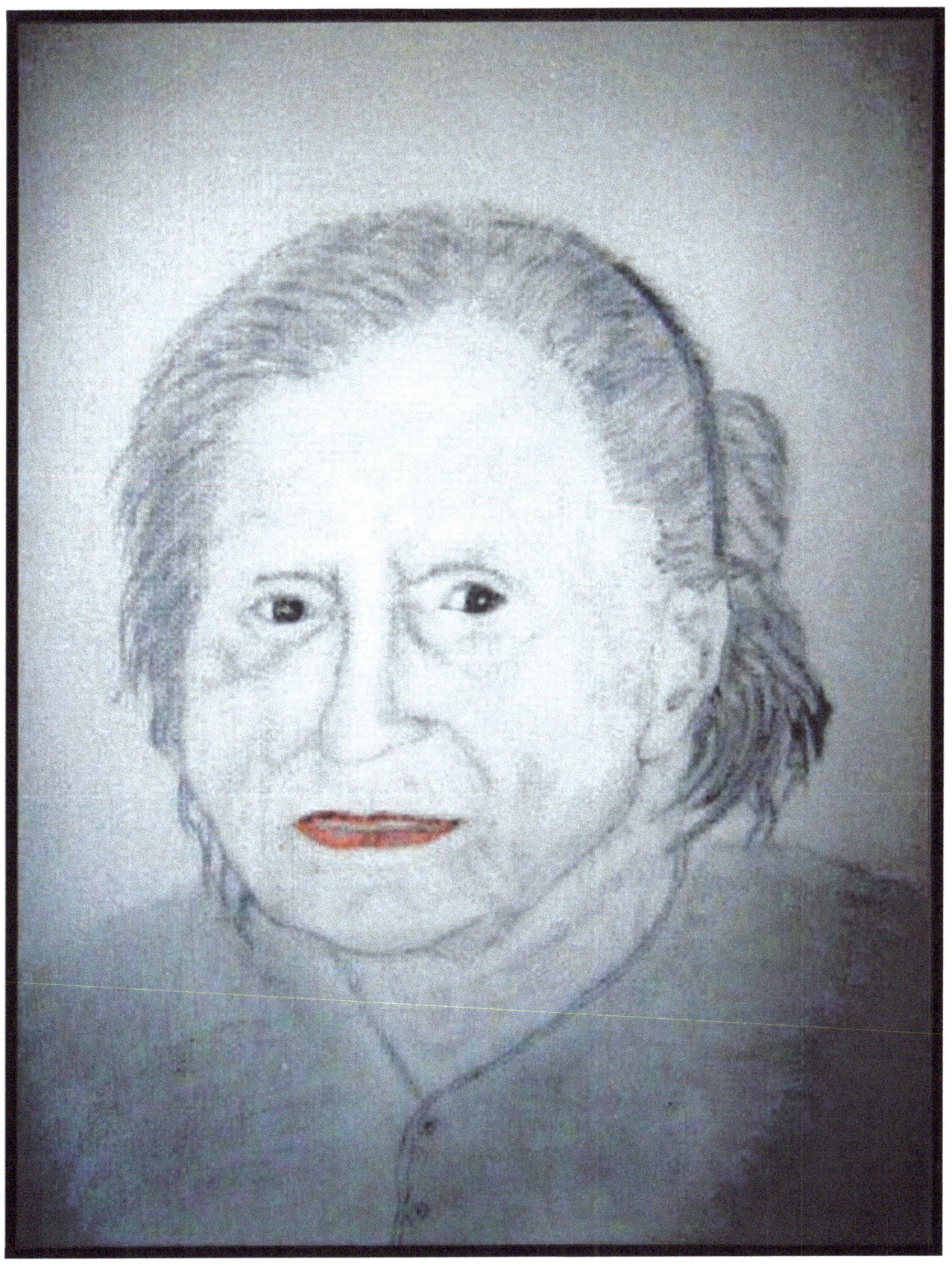

A TOUCH OF GOLDEN
(An Ode To Mom & Dad)

Fifty years and a thousand
or so tears, are what a
wedding anniversary holds.

Life's been oh so wonderful,
oh so sweet.

And, now it's a 'touch of golden'.

Your lives have been full, oh
so complete, you've tasted
life's bittersweet melody.

With twelve marvelous children,
so many grandchildren and great grandchildren, you've had God's blessing.

We've had your blessing.

Sweet memories of good times gone by,
remembering the downfalls too,
but cherishing it all, through and through.

You've made us all appreciate and understand,
the meaning of Love, the true meaning of Life.

And, you are the Love of our Life.

It's been a touch of golden, yes, fifty years,
But your golden years are only about to begin,
Yes, fifty years and a thousand or so tears.

God Bless your anniversary and God Bless You.
I love you (we love you).

Splish!

RETURN JOURNEY

I, the one that is born,
I the one that breathes,
I, the one that lives,
I, the one that dies,
I, the one that is reborn!

CHAPTER 4

Poetic I be!

READER'S PARTICIPATION PAGE

(if you so choose)

What one gets out of a poem might be neither here nor there, but is of great value in understanding one's self – your emotions and basic outlooks on life are important to your thought process.

What did each poem mean to you when you read them?

Perhaps you need to read them a few times.

Refer back to the **INTRO** for a description of what certain poems might mean. Remember, not all poems will stress a true meaning; after all, they say *poetry is what it is!*

I'm sure you've noticed that not all poems are happy, not all are long and some may not even rhyme, but that's what it means when they say 'it is what it is' – putting ideas, thoughts and emotions, all in writing, to share (or not).

You may have understood some poems immediately, some maybe not, so use this page to analyze the poems, who knows, your analysis may in turn help you to some extent. And, remember, there are really no wrong answers; you are your own judge.

PAGE	POEM TITLE	YOUR ANALYSIS?
26	The Pain	
28	Time, Only Time *(part one)*	
30	Time, Only Time *(part two)*	
32	Unseen Scars	
34	Home	
36	What My Eyes See	
38	If The Morning Doesn't Come	
40	The Cottage	
42	Shadow Of Darkness	
44	Beyond The Unknown	
46	Shadow Of Fear	
48	Silent Waves	
50	Love Can Hurt	
52	The Visitors	
54	Some Kind Of High	
56	My Brother and I …	
58	The Reflection	
60	A Ray Of Hope	
62	The Depths Of Your Mind	
64	Life Or Death?	
66	From Beyond	
68	Visions Drifting rough	
70	Envision Me	
72	Why?	
74	Fortunate To Be One	
76	Love's Pain	
78	Fears Within *(part one)*	
80	Fears Within *(part two)*	
82	Wanting Her	
84	Temper, Temper	
86	Just A Face	
88	Only You Can	
90	Down and Out	
92	Confusion	
94	For You I'll Wait	
96	That Feeling	
98	A *Touch Of Golden* (Ode To Mom and Dad)	
100	Return Journey	

AFTERWORD

Guilt Factors
~ Mind Games & 'ought Nots! ~

Chapter 1 was written from a layman's point of view with a motivational spirit. It was never intended to capture the complete subject matter, professionally or otherwise, only to focus on its existence and seek out some positives.

Chapter 2 was inserted to specifically give you historical views (quotes) on the subject of guilt and the workings of the mind.

Chapter 3 the mainstay, is a compilation of poetry and artwork, and is what it is.

Chapter 4 is a reader's participation area where you can decipher the meaning of each poem, if you so wish. Sometimes when you read a poem it may leave you a little bewildered as to what it could possibly mean, while some can be quite obvious. From Shakespeare: *'Who understandeth thee?'*.

Always stay positive, believe in yourself, dreams can come true!

Robert R. Blondin

bobmeistersplace.com
bobmeisterb@gmail.com